Little Gems

For Business and Life

Success leaves a trail of clues.
Wherever you find yourself on your journey to success,
these gems are here to enhance your path.

By
JOHN RYDELL III

Copyright © 2024 by John Rydell III. All rights reserved.

All text and concepts are bound by the international copyright laws.

ISBN: 9798324656669

Published in the United States of America

Book by John Rydell III.

Learn more at www.LittleGems.io

PREFACE

Years ago I was involved in the opening of a new restaurant in Orange County. One of the original menu items that still lives on today was called "The Little Gems Salad." The salad was handcrafted and fresh; nothing came from a jar. I loved it. Amidst a nice bed of lettuce, I could dig through the salad with my fork and find little gems of shrimp, crab, lobster, avocado, and croutons – all topped with a green goddess dressing. I always assumed that the salad was called "Little Gems" because of the little gems of seafood I could find with my fork.

I'm embarrassed to admit that it wasn't until years later that I learned that the salad had a creative double meaning. It turns out that little gems is the type of lettuce that was used – not just the name of the nuggets of goodness that I hunted for at lunch!

When choosing a name for this book I kept coming back to little gems. Just like the salad, the ideas in this book have been handcrafted. In the everyday 'lettuce' that sustains us, we uncover little gems of wisdom.

In this first volume, I've put together more than 200 little gems for business and life that I have collected. I know there are thousands of additional little gems waiting to be curated into different future collections. What might those be? Little Gems for Children, Little Gems for Parents, Little Gems for

Couples, Little Gems for Finance, Little Gems for Startups, Little Gems for Athletes. The possibilities are endless. If you have any Little Gems that you think belong in future collections, I welcome your contributions. You can always find me at jrydell@gmail.com.

Just like me, many of the humans I pulled these Little Gems from are flawed. But that doesn't mean we can't learn from them. In other words, just because I'm quoting someone or sourcing them doesn't mean that I agree with everything else they have said or done in their life. As my friend Jon Fleishman says, "If good people can sometimes do bad things, then it must also be true that bad people can sometimes do good things…"

And finally, a big thank you to the amazing people in my life who have helped me find these Little Gems over the past 53 years. My friends, family, business colleagues, mentors, and authors have all contributed to making me the person that I am. Where possible, I've given credit to the people who originated these little gems.

Enjoy The Little Gems!

JR

BY JOHN RYDELL III

💎 Why Little Gems are good for you.

"I constantly see people rise in life who are not the smartest, sometimes even the most diligent, but they are learning machines. They go to bed every night a little bit wiser than when they got up and boy does that help–particularly when you have a long run ahead of you."

Charlie Munger.

💎 Be kind and direct.

Everyone wants someone who is nice to them.

But everyone is scared to tell the truth.

Be the person who is both — be kind AND direct.

BY JOHN RYDELL III

💎 Have goals!

Successful people write down their goals and review them often.

Find a way to do this physically or digitally. Every day.

LITTLE GEMS FOR BUSINESS AND LIFE

💎 The early bird gets the worm.

Be at work before others.

I'm typing this at 4:18 am on a Wednesday morning.

BY JOHN RYDELL III

💎 There is no "fair and balanced."

So, read news sources of all types to understand both positions and make up your own mind.

Every morning I have the news digitally to me delivered from a wide range of sources – from far left to far right.

◆ Life isn't fair. Don't expect it to be.

If you are reading this book, then you likely don't want life to be fair.

The global average income is somewhere around $10,000.

Nearly half of the people alive today live on less than a few dollars per day.

Stop believing life is fair – it isn't.

BY JOHN RYDELL III

♦ **Physical exercise is important.**

Find something you love to do.

Get in the habit.

Exercise makes you mentally and physically healthier.

AND it prepares you to deal with the stress of battle.

♦ Stay ahead of your team.

Always stay one step ahead of the people who work for you.

While working today, make sure you know what you have to do tomorrow.

When you are working tomorrow, make sure you know what you have to do next week.

Use a system to carefully track appointments, tasks, and action items.

BY JOHN RYDELL III

💎 Be responsible when you travel.

If you are going out of town, make sure your tasks are covered.

And set the right expectations ahead of time about when you can be interrupted on vacation.

Set it all up the right way before you leave, and then go have a great time.

💎 "Early is on time!"

Don't be late.

If you are going to be a little late, tell everyone.

Don't be rude.

BY JOHN RYDELL III

💎 Don't keep people waiting!

My friend Dr. Mark Redd is one of the best periodontists in the world.

He could keep his patients waiting forever. But he refuses to do that.

When you walk into the door of his office, there is a reception area – NOT a waiting room.

Honor people's time.

◆ Write stuff down.

It drives me nuts when someone says they are going to do something, but they don't write it down.

Write down everything... preferably in a computer or a system where you will not forget.

Writing things down helps you commit to getting them done.

If you try to just remember what you are supposed to do, you have no chance.

BY JOHN RYDELL III

💎 Don't get paid per hour.

Whenever possible, generate income that doesn't require your ongoing time.

Otherwise going on vacation is never fun... and you'll never be rich.

$1,000/hr makes you about $1mm per year after overhead.

♦ Cash flow matters.

Don't get caught up in fancy EBITDA-based or accrual-based accounting.

Always know how much cash your business has and how much you are making every month.

Cash is king. Board members should know this… always.

BY JOHN RYDELL III

💎 The room where it happens.

What is it like in a room full of the most powerful people in the world?

Surprisingly normal. Casual. Fun. Youthful.

Don't think you need to be stuffy and formal to impress.

◆ Modest people are the successful ones.

If you meet someone who boasts about their success, they usually aren't very successful.

If you meet someone who downplays their success, they are often massively successful.

The same is true for parents bragging about their children.

BY JOHN RYDELL III

💎 Network like Zack.

A huge percentage of the people who work at my company can be traced back to Zack.

He spends the time to know people virtually. But he doesn't show up at many cocktail parties.

And never networks in a cringy way.

He just delivers value, is nice, helps people, and connects them.

♦ The Longenecker rule:

My friend Phil knew how to be a great host.

He always picked up the tab.

He even moved his belongings out of his primary bedroom once at his house, so I could stay in it while he stayed in a tiny room in the back.

BY JOHN RYDELL III

◆ The Jeff Higashi Rule:

Buy people a beer.

Only costs a few dollars but everyone will love you.

Never expect anything in return.

◆ Do something you love!

You are going to spend more time working than anything else in life.

If you don't love what you are doing, find something else to do.

Life's too short.

BY JOHN RYDELL III

💎 Nobody should be surprised when they get fired.

If someone is underperforming or their job is in jeopardy, tell them very directly.

We are often too polite and then an employee is surprised when they are fired.

The kindest thing you can do is to be super direct about the danger they are in.

◆ Over-communicate.

Oftentimes communication is more important than even doing work.

If people don't know what you are doing for them, they assume you aren't doing anything.

BY JOHN RYDELL III

💎 Don't have an assistant who just slows you down.

Make your own decisions. Create your own calendar and travel plans.

Have an assistant do things that help you speed up, stay organized, and don't require your input.

💎 Delegate everything that you possibly can.

Delegate tasks to others, unless the tasks are of super high value.

Even if they only do it 80% as well as you, that's ok because they have more time to pay attention.

You need to be working on more important things that only you can do.

Why are you doing $20/hr work if you are the CEO?

BY JOHN RYDELL III

💎 Don't let your talent go to waste.

If you have a unique talent that will help you change the world, you must pursue it.

Any time you spend on something else is stealing from future generations.

💎 Elon Musk on doing good:

"What I care about is the reality of goodness,

Not the perception of it.

And what I see all over the place

Is people who care about LOOKING good, while doing EVIL.

F*ck them!"

Quoted from a verbal interview at NYT Dealbook Summit, 2023.

BY JOHN RYDELL III

💎 10% Rule:

Want to make your business 2x better?

Find 10 things and improve them all by 10%.

WOW! Now do it again.

◆ What's the ROI?

Measure the return on investment for all projects and hiring decisions.

If you can't make a simple justification for the project or person, do something else.

BY JOHN RYDELL III

◆ Create scorecards.

Want to know how you are doing with the ROI of your projects and investments?

Require the leader of the project to do a scorecard when the project is done.

Review the initial project estimate, projected ROI, and see how you did.

◆ Find peace with your investment strategy.

There are lots of personal investment strategies that work.

But none is perfect.

You must find one that will work for you in the good times and the bad and stick with it.

Otherwise you chase what's hot and always lose in the end.

BY JOHN RYDELL III

♦ Compound your money and your business.

$100,000 grows to nearly $2mm @ 10% for 30 years.

A $1mm business grows to nearly $40mm @ 20% for 30 years.

You can have a GIANT business by growing 20% consistently for a long time.

💎 Compound your skills.

Get 1% better every day at something.

Before you know it, you will be a master.

💎 Everyone is often wrong.

When "everyone" believes something is going to happen, they are usually wrong.

The mob mentality is usually wrong, especially when it comes to investing.

Don't get caught up following the mob.

♦ Be an orange.

If everyone else is an apple, then be an orange.

Stand out from the crowd. Do something different. You'll get noticed.

BY JOHN RYDELL III

💎 Rydell rule #1.

Reply to every email within 1 business day.

Demand the same of your team.

It will change your business and your life.

💎 Sort your emails.

Take the time to make a Gmail rule to filter out all non-urgent emails so they don't land in your inbox.

Then you can read and archive all of those emails super quickly 1-2 times per day without being distracted all day.

Some people like Superhuman for this. I use Gmail. Nice and easy.

BY JOHN RYDELL III

💎 CEOs should be accessible.

A CEO should always be available to the team... at least via email.

A leader can't spend the day talking to everyone all of the time.

But a CEO can surely invite feedback and comments via email.

I wrote Mark Cuban an email one day. He wrote back within an hour – personally.

💎 Don't use fancy writing.

See this book? Do I use lots of fancy words?

Do I try to sound smart?

Or do I write with small sentences and short descriptions?

BY JOHN RYDELL III

💎 What I learned in 7th grade.

My 7th grade middle school English teacher, Mr Conway, taught the class:

A paper (or speech) should be like a skirt.

It should be long enough to cover the subject but short enough to be interesting.

That's the only thing I remember from the class.

💎 Bequer rule:

I have a friend named Benjamin Bequer. He is a successful entrepreneur.

He hates listening to people talk about stuff that doesn't matter.

Create a culture where if you don't have anything to say, it is ok to stay silent.

BY JOHN RYDELL III

💎 **Have a higher purpose.**

Your business needs a purpose.

Your life needs a purpose.

Find one.

Commit to it.

Suggestion: Read my rhyming children's book about Jesus.

💎 "Attack each day with an enthusiasm unknown to mankind."

Each day is a gift. Go see what you can get done today. Attack.

Create the life you want. Today.

From Jim Harbaugh - NFL player and coach.

BY JOHN RYDELL III

💎 Be thankful for the assist.

"Always give props to the guy who made the assist – The player who made the shot already knows he is good."

(Rough paraphrase from S6Ep4 of the Billions tv show.)

💎 My dad is an attorney.

He taught me:

Don't get in legal fights.

Be in the business of business. Don't be in the business of suing people.

Only the lawyers win. Especially in divorce and breakups.

BY JOHN RYDELL III

♦ **A Hug.**

From *The Boy, the Mole, the Fox, and the Horse* by Charlie Mackesy

"I've discovered something better than cake."

"No you haven't," said the boy.

"I have," replied the mole.

"What is it?"

"A hug. It lasts longer."

◆ Call your mom.

Just remember how much you like it when you get a loving call from your kids.

Remember that your mom probably wants to hear from YOU.

So be nice. And call your mom. Tell her you love her.

She gave you life.

BY JOHN RYDELL III

💎　Write thank you notes.

Hand write them.

This is a dying art. If you do it, you will stand out.

Especially when you are interviewing.

There are still hiring managers who will NOT hire someone who doesn't write a hand-written thank you.

💎 Hire people who deliver results.

Get rid of people in the middle who just generate reports and make people feel good.

Everyone should personally deliver an ROI for the company.

BY JOHN RYDELL III

💎 Secretaries will hire secretaries.

This is not a joke. Get too big and the next thing you know a department will need its own HR, its own legal, its own finance, and its own IT.

And in the end secretaries will need secretaries and nobody will be working on the core anymore.

Stop it!

◆ Forgive people.

Not for their benefit, but for yours.

BY JOHN RYDELL III

💎 Be a great loyal business partner.

There are very few great partners and partnerships.

Always do what you say you will do for your partners.

Communicate often. Work through hard issues.

A truly great partnership can be beneficial to both parties.

◆ Pay your bills on time.

If you say you are going to pay someone, do it on time or early.

Expect the same from others.

Negotiate to pay less if you always pay fast.

BY JOHN RYDELL III

💎 Pay people based on performance.

Whenever possible, tie compensation to performance.

The closer you can make it to what they can control, the better.

Don't wimp out and just pay flat salaries or tie comp to the overall business.

💎 Nobody cares about a business like an owner.

This is just the truth.

Don't expect others to care as much as you do if you are an owner.

BY JOHN RYDELL III

💎 Nobody knows what they are doing.

Just go for it and don't be scared.

LITTLE GEMS FOR BUSINESS AND LIFE

◆ From a Facebook poster:

"What would you do if you weren't afraid?"

Attributed to Dan Rose (Twitter @DanRose999)

BY JOHN RYDELL III

💎 Play Boldly!

When I'm playing competitive golf I use a golf ball that says PLAY BOLDLY.

Arnold Palmer would say "You must play boldly to win."

In golf (and in life) you don't win if you play conservatively.

You win when you are bold. Play boldly!

💎 "Shupersize" your event.

My friend Brad Shupe has been the GM of many great country clubs.

He constantly challenges his team to "supersize" their events.

He challenges them to figure out how to make each event even more special or unique or better.

The results are magical.

BY JOHN RYDELL III

💎 Be funny & have fun.

You aren't doing brain surgery.

Nobody is going to die.

Lighten up.

♦ Own your youth.

The tech billionaires made it ok to be young so use it to your advantage.

Don't worry if you look young or if you are young.

But if you are young, find a wise old mentor. Then you'll crush it.

BY JOHN RYDELL III

💎 Boobs sell.

Sex sells.

Is this PC? No.

Is it honest and important? Yes.

◆ Have a board.

But don't waste a ton of time doing prep work for the board members.

Some businesses spend more time prepping for board meetings than they do working.

Ugh. Don't do that.

Board members – don't waste your company's time.

BY JOHN RYDELL III

💎 Real businesses make money.

The way you can tell if a business is delivering value is if it makes money consistently over time.

Don't forget that during manias.

◆ Keep compensation plans simple.

When they get too complex, people find loopholes and forget what is most important.

BY JOHN RYDELL III

♦ Have hard conversations while they are easy.

Hard conversations are way easier at the beginning when you don't think bad stuff will happen to your relationship.

So have them early.

For example, "What happens if business fails? If someone dies? If an employee or customer quits?"

♦ Don't fight the trend.

Trends do matter and they last longer than you think they will.

So follow trends and be aware of them.

But when a trend turns, reverse course and get out of the way quickly.

BY JOHN RYDELL III

💎 Invest the opposite of what you hear at the golf course!

(Same can be applied to large Thanksgiving dinners.)

When "everyone" at the golf course is telling you to invest in something, run fast!

Do the opposite.

◆ The Paul Brady Rule:

I have a friend named Paul Brady. He is a successful investor.

He loves a great debate and he loves challenging decisions.

But when his team builds consensus to go in a different direction, he falls in line 100% and never fights again.

Hubspot sums this up as, "Debate. Decide. Commit."

BY JOHN RYDELL III

♦ Divine Fortune:

"As luck would have it, God was with us."

Mind blowing.

◆ Rich Meyer on parenting:

"Being a good parent is becoming well-versed in navigating the art of freedom with your children.

Remember - you aren't raising children. You are forming future adults.

By the time they leave your home, they should have had plenty of practice making their own decisions and solving their own problems – whatever the consequences."

Rich is the father of 8 and the president of JSerra Catholic HS in San Juan Capistrano.

BY JOHN RYDELL III

💎 Raising children is hard.

It is especially hard when they are young and you aren't sleeping much.

The kindest, nicest, most loving people in the world are going to be irritated when they don't sleep.

Of course relationships are going to be strained during those times. Embrace it.

◈ Sexist relationship advice.

Here is some completely sexist (but real) relationship advice:

Men - do more domestic work than you want to.

Women - give your spouse more physical love than you want to.

But never expect anything in return.

BY JOHN RYDELL III

💎 Your child does get enough playing time.

If your kid gets slightly less playing time than you think they deserve on their sports team...

Then the coach is probably giving them just the right amount of playing time.

💎 You do make enough money.

If you make slightly less money than you think you deserve...

Then you are getting paid correctly.

BY JOHN RYDELL III

💎 Give money to charity. Give lots.

And measure the results and how it makes you feel.

The richest people in the world are often great at giving.

If you don't expect the money to come back to you, then it will, many times over.

♦ Charity match 2:1.

Don't try to pick which charities your company cares most about.

Avoid playing favorites among your staff. Set up a matching giving program.

It will reward your staff for the things they are involved with. Their skin is in the game.

BY JOHN RYDELL III

💎 Sweep the floors.

Be a servant leader.

Delegation is important but some days you have to jump in and sweep the floors.

No job should be beneath the leader when it has to get done.

◆ If you own something, you care more.

So make your employees owners whenever you can.

BY JOHN RYDELL III

💎 Be pleased but not satisfied.

Make sure people know that you are pleased with the job they are doing.

Then talk about how you can help them do even better.

If you forget to tell them that you are pleased, then they will think you are never happy.

♦ Don't make too many rules.

Rules drive people crazy. And they slow you down.

Have as few as possible.

Focus on doing the right thing; not making stupid rules to follow.

BY JOHN RYDELL III

💎 Don't break the law. Period.

However, the more complex your business gets, the more you realize that tax and legal and compliance are complicated.

So find trusted accountants and lawyers who will help you. But don't let them ruin the business by trying to be perfect.

Small companies have a huge advantage because they don't have expensive attorneys who say no.

♦ Lawyers should write down agreements made by others.

Business people should hash out business terms.

Have the hard conversations.

Then ask the lawyers to write it all down.

Avoid using lawyers as negotiators except in rare circumstances.

BY JOHN RYDELL III

💎 Herb Cohen rule:

To negotiate, you have to "Care... but not THAT much."

Everything in life is negotiable.

But remember if you negotiate too well and pay too little, then nobody wants to be your employee or your partner.

◆ Negotiate with fractions of a penny.

Don't price stuff at $10 or $20.

Don't even price it at $10.23.

When you get to real negotiation, use fractions of a penny.

Then the other side will know (or think) you are serious.

BY JOHN RYDELL III

💎 Nerves are just your body getting you ready.

Are you scared to present in public? Feeling nervous?

Perfect. That's just your body preparing you to do an awesome job.

◆ President Reagan was known as the great communicator.

He also brought people together.

It is hard to imagine in today's world, but in 1984 he won 49 out of 50 states.

YouTube is filled with videos of his speeches for you to review and learn from.

BY JOHN RYDELL III

💎 "Talk Less... Smile More."

From the musical Hamilton.

💎 The Margaret Mead Rule:

"Never doubt that a small group of thoughtful citizens can change the world; indeed, it's the only thing that ever has."

Little groups can crush big organizations. Never forget that.

BY JOHN RYDELL III

💎 Money and time are always limited.

No department ever has enough money or time to do everything.

Your goal as a manager is to prioritize and say no to things that won't make a big difference.

💎 Projects can only have one owner.

Never have co-owners of projects.

Everything needs ONE owner.

That owner can have a team.

BY JOHN RYDELL III

◆ **People work based on how they get paid.**

So be careful how you set up incentive plans.

People will always work to maximize their comp plan.

Even if they seem like altruistic people, they care about themselves first.

💎 Use deadlines.

Without deadlines, nothing gets done.

With deadlines, people work with urgency.

But never make up a fake deadline that you forget about.

BY JOHN RYDELL III

💎 Meetings are super expensive.

People with limited spending authority are allowed to schedule recurring wasteful meetings with tons of people.

You'd never let that person waste all of the money if they asked for it. Don't let them waste it scheduling unnecessary meetings that last too long.

◆ Budgets suck.

Never trust a budget. (Certainly not a federal government budget.)

Creating budgets is a good idea.

But don't blindly stick to it unless it is working great.

Always be ready to pivot and react on the fly.

Organizations that simply "meet budget" by year-end aren't reacting properly to the dozens of things that happen all year long.

BY JOHN RYDELL III

💎 Projections are BS.

Any time you see a projection for the future of a business, be VERY wary.

People creating future projections are often just creating models that they hope they can defend.

Often they are built backwards...starting with the answer they want.

Modeling is fine but don't spend too much time creating models and certainly don't trust them.

💎 Have midwest values.

Even if you are a Silicon Valley tech company.

Treat people right. Keep things simple.

Do what you say you are going to do.

Don't be flashy.

BY JOHN RYDELL III

💎 Lots of people who appear rich are not.

Don't assume a rich person will pay on time.

Value people who honor their commitments and pay on time.

They are few and far between.

💎 Find some friends.

Very few people have lots of friends.

Most people are lucky enough to have a few great ones. You don't need many.

I pray you find some. And that your kids do also.

When you do, treasure them.

BY JOHN RYDELL III

💎 Read books. Especially this one.

Find stuff you love to read. And dig in.

It is good for your life, your business, and your soul.

♦ The 4th Commandment:

"Remember the sabbath day."

God didn't make this commandment because he needed a day of rest.

He did it because humans need a regular time of rest.

And it was so important that it became the 4th commandment.

Want to modernize it? Put away your cellphone one day per week.

BY JOHN RYDELL III

💎 The Chris Ledyard Rule:

"Pray like it is up to God. But work like it is up to you."

Enough said.

◆ Farah Pandith's call to action:

Farah is an extremely smart person who has been fighting violent extremism for a long time.

She is a deep thinker about complex problems. She has traveled to 80+ countries.

But when I asked her what a room full of people could actually do immediately to help, she said:

"Go out of your way to smile and say hi to everyone you see... especially the invisible people."

Sometimes you have to take big, complex problems and give people a small tangible step to take.

BY JOHN RYDELL III

♦ The Mark Surfas Rule:

Birthdays matter

Birthdays can be lonely. Other than facebook and a few texts, people realize on their special day that not many others know and care.

So be a person who does know and care. Be great at celebrating birthdays.

💎 Treasure your liberty if you have it.

In the US, we have a whole statue to remind us about the importance of liberty.

Having freedom of your way of life, behavior, and political views is a great gift.

Don't take it for granted.

BY JOHN RYDELL III

💎 Government doesn't solve problems.

America was built on the notion that the citizens are in charge.

And that citizens would fix their own problems.

Government (especially big government) is at best inefficient and wasteful.

💎 Fire and wood.

"If that doesn't light your fire, then your wood is wet."

Great line. Can be applied to life, business, emotion, religion, and actual fires.

BY JOHN RYDELL III

♦ Anniversaries matter.

Your wedding anniversary is important. Hopefully you know that!

But work anniversaries matter also. They are an opportunity to acknowledge longevity and commitment.

They are a time to say THANK YOU — not congratulations.

Working at your company and keeping a job should be thanked.

If you congratulate someone, you are telling everyone else that it is hard to work at the company for a long time.

💎 Don't let projects take forever.

You could get married tomorrow. Or it could take a year of stress.

Projects grow to fill the allowed time. Don't let them.

Seriously. You could plan a great wedding and get married tomorrow.

Or you could spend 2 years planning a wedding, be stressed out, and still get basically the same result.

BY JOHN RYDELL III

💎 Want to find a good spouse?

Choose someone you can talk to for the rest of your life.

And it doesn't hurt if you like listening to them as well.

◆ Find something you like to do nightly to relax with your spouse.

Lisa and I enjoy watching some mindless TV at the end of the day – together.

Others enjoy a crossword puzzle or reading the same book.

But find a way to be together doing something that brings you both joy.

BY JOHN RYDELL III

◆ Create one-take updates.

(I call these videos 'Rydell Raw.' Go create your own 'raw' brand.)

When it comes time to make a video update for the company, just do it in one take.

You'll never make a perfect video and they cost too much to try to perfect.

So build a culture where people do their best and do everything in one take.

It makes the videos more real, more raw, and a heck of a lot cheaper.

Similarly - don't make Powerpoint presentations that look good but the content sucks.

◈ Reach out to your CEO (and/or boss).

Ask questions, be supportive, provide kind feedback.

Almost nobody does. You will stand out.

BY JOHN RYDELL III

💎 Bring solutions to your boss.

Not problems.

💎 You always see a manager on the floor at great restaurants.

Having a manager constantly visible ensures everyone is doing a great job.

It ensures that the staff knows that management cares about every detail.

It provides great teaching opportunities.

You can apply this to any business – not just restaurants.

To see this in action go visit Zuma in Vegas and watch Ayo Onayemi work his magic.

BY JOHN RYDELL III

💎 Bots dominate social media and reviews.

So don't assume the noise you see and read online is from real people.

Bots, evil people, and extremists on both sides are the ones who post comments.

Don't forget the 70% who are silent in the middle.

💎 The Gavin Newsom rule:

I might get in trouble for this one.

Gavin Newsom is a genius politician.

He will tell you to your face what you want to hear and make you believe it.

But as soon as you turn around, he'll do what is in his own best interest.

He isn't the only one. Just the most masterful one I've met.

BY JOHN RYDELL III

◆ Be skeptical of the news and what you read online.

(Whether you are on the right or the left!)

When you read news articles about things you know first hand, you realize how many mistakes there are.

So apply that filter to all articles and be careful trusting what you read unless you know the source.

💎 Mental health is important.

Talk about mental health like you do about physical health. No stigmas.

Accommodate people who need help. But don't just let people make excuses.

BY JOHN RYDELL III

◆ Don't cheat. Ever.

Don't ever cheat a customer, or an employee, or a business partner. (OR your spouse!)

♦ Loyalty matters.

Be loyal to your early customers, your early staff, and your early vendors.

People who took a risk on you deserve your loyalty long after you may no longer need them.

BY JOHN RYDELL III

💎 It is good to work with friends and family.

But go overboard setting expectations before you do.

When things go wrong with friends and family, it gets really, really hard.

💎 Hire people who have great networks.

If you are hiring a manager, they should immediately know people they will recruit to join your team.

If a manager of people doesn't have a network of people to bring with them, something is wrong. Don't hire them.

BY JOHN RYDELL III

◈ **Hire slow. Fire fast.**

Sounds harsh. But it is reality.

I never hear anyone say, "I sure wish XXXX person was still here and that I hadn't fired them so fast."

◆ Work from home. But do it right.

I have run a virtual company for more than 20 years.

Working from home allows people to have a great lifestyle, not spend time in traffic, and is better for the planet.

In trade, people who work from home have to be disciplined and work their butts off given the great flexible advantages they are given.

If you think working from home means you have an easy job, your job or company is in jeopardy.

BY JOHN RYDELL III

💎 Get rid of people who stir up trouble.

If an employee is a pain in the neck and makes life hard for everyone else, get rid of them.

If they are kind and direct and point out problems and solutions, treasure them.

💎 Don't be scared to let employees go.

When an employee is let go because they aren't a fit, it usually works out better for that person long-term anyway.

So don't wait. Get rid of people who don't belong.

You will be doing your company a favor and often doing the employee a favor as well.

BY JOHN RYDELL III

💎 Don't let tech people have control.

I am a tech person. I have a computer science degree.

Tech people can rule the company and can tell you what is possible and what isn't.

Don't let them. They get to collaborate on decisions. Not control them.

💎 Your own shit DOES stink!

Programmers think their code won't have bugs.

Writers think their writing won't need editing.

Be humble. And find good people to help you test and proofread!

BY JOHN RYDELL III

💎 Build what you actually need and want.

The best products are built by people who are building something they personally need and want to use.

It is so much easier when everyone involved is eating their own dog food.

If you aren't building something you will personally use, then you better have a customer close to you giving real feedback.

💎 Giant companies are very rare.

Don't compare the reality of your company with the giant public companies.

You can have an amazing company and still not be Microsoft, Amazon, Apple, or Nvidia.

Also remember that they were not overnight success stories.

BY JOHN RYDELL III

💎 When the grass is greener, water your own lawn.

If your neighbor's grass looks greener than yours, don't be jealous. Fix your own.

The same is true for your business and your relationships.

Don't worry. Everything isn't perfect at your neighbor's house either.

💎 Social media doesn't tell the whole story.

Don't compare your normal life to someone else's best day on social media.

People only post on social media when they are having one of the most interesting days of their lives.

The pictures are filtered. They are on vacation. They all look happy.

Do NOT for one instant think that is what their real life is like. It isn't.

BY JOHN RYDELL III

💎 Augusta National looks perfect on TV during the Masters.

The place is truly amazing.

But do you know the course is closed all summer?

That's because they can't be great 365 days per year.

They know their goal is to be perfect in spring. Not every day.

◆ The Tiger, LeBron, Kobe Rule:

Even if you are the best, outwork everyone else.

Hmmm... maybe that is why they all were the best?

BY JOHN RYDELL III

💎 The Steph Curry Rule:

Have joy like a kid on a basketball court.

Never forget to have fun.

Never forget the joy of a child.

Joy is infectious.

◆ Sports betting and gambling are HUGE.

But Vegas wasn't built by losing bets.

Never bet more than you can afford to lose.

And remember that the very, very best professional sports bettors win about 58% of their bets.

@TheSharpPlays on X for some free advice and lessons from an insider.

BY JOHN RYDELL III

♦ Forums are great. Coaches are better.

Executive forums can be great. But they can also be a huge waste of time with the wrong people.

One-on-one coaching can be even more amazing if you find the right coach or mentor and take it seriously.

I have had success with both.

◆ Coaching advice from the greatest coach ever:

"A coach is someone who can give correction, without causing resentment."

John Wooden

BY JOHN RYDELL III

💎 The Jeff Olson Rule:

"Any time you see what looks like a breakthrough, it is always the end result of a long series of little things, done consistently right over time."

Jeff Olson, The Slight Edge

💎 Create a BAR!

(Short for Big Ass Report).

We update our company BAR every week and review it for at least 20 min.

It gives you the ability to make sure you never lose focus on what is most important.

It uncovers problems. Just the act of updating the BAR forces people to own the metrics.

BY JOHN RYDELL III

💎 People love transparency.

Be as transparent as possible with your team, your customers, and your community.

Transparency doesn't scare people. It gives them information and makes them trust you.

💎 Focus on revenue-producing activities.

Don't confuse action with results.

Don't just look busy.

Do stuff that matters and brings in revenue.

Sharpening your pencils and organizing your desk doesn't make you any money!

BY JOHN RYDELL III

💎 Sell by solving problems.

Don't try to "convince" someone to buy your product or service.

It is way better to understand their problem and show how your solution will help.

♦ Sell with your personality.

Some people sell with emotion.

Some sell with facts.

Some with hard work.

Sell the way that is natural for your personality.

Don't be someone else. It won't work.

BY JOHN RYDELL III

💎 Always be selling.

Selling is part of life and part of every job.

No matter who you are, keep selling.

But never be annoying.

Great salespeople are so good that you don't even know they are selling you something.

💎 Find a way to listen to feedback.

But not if it eats you alive.

As a leader, you have to know what your customers think.

So find a way to get honest feedback.

Remember that the internet is filled with haters and bots that are out to get you.

But you still have to filter through that to find the truth without much filtering or you lose the core.

BY JOHN RYDELL III

💎 Keep bureaucracy out!

Do not let your company be overrun with rules and too much hierarchy.

Some rules are important. But the fewer the better.

♦ Streamline approval processes.

Don't make people get approval for little things that reports will reveal later.

If small decisions or expenses will show up in monthly reports, then stop making people get approval for little things.

There is a story about Bill Gates submitting expense reports when he was worth billions. Stupid.

BY JOHN RYDELL III

💎 **Spend your company's money like it is your own.**

In fact, spend the company's money MORE carefully than your own.

Always be happy to justify every dollar spent.

Sometimes you make financial mistakes. Own them.

💎 Have you watched Jiro Dreams of Sushi?

It is a documentary about a master sushi chef in Japan.

He passionately loves his job.

His dedication to excellence is unmatched.

He doesn't get distracted from his core.

His attention to detail is awe-inspiring.

BY JOHN RYDELL III

💎 All about puffery.

I love to exaggerate stories. It makes them fun to tell.

But when you start exaggerating things that matter, eventually nobody believes you.

💎 Compliance sucks.

Nobody likes dealing with compliance but most companies need it.

We call it "trust and safety" to try to help our team and our customers know that we are doing it for them.

BY JOHN RYDELL III

Lifetime value of a customer.

Always measure the lifetime value of a customer.

It is the only way to make good decisions about investments in sales and marketing.

If your lifetime value is low, go to work and make it higher.

♦ What is the asset value of your business?

If your business is worth $10mm, it better yield you $1mm/yr or more.

If it doesn't, then sell it like you would any under-performing asset.

BY JOHN RYDELL III

💎 The Scott Olivet rule:

Decide if something is an 80% project or a 100% project.

When you embark on a project, are you trying to get it 80% good but get it out fast?

Or are you going to wait for 100% perfection even if that takes a really long time and a lot of money.

Both strategies can work but you need to know which one you are using.

♦ Add ritual to your business.

Do you celebrate birthdays? Do you give out special appreciation for big work anniversaries?

Do you always start your big meetings with inspirational music or a joke?

Have some rituals. It makes work feel more sacred. But don't creep people out and look like a cult!

BY JOHN RYDELL III

◆ **Honey Badgers are badass. And so is Randall the narrator.**

Search YouTube for "Randall honey badger."

💎 The Nick Saban "and or but" rule:

When prepping for the NFL draft, the staff talks about all of a player's qualifications.

Then they either say "AND he's a great guy" or "AND he is a leader, "etc.

OR they say "BUT he doesn't listen or "BUT he doesn't work hard, " etc.

When companies (or teams) are hiring, they want ANDS – not BUTS!

How are you going to edit your behavior so that you have an AND and not a BUT?

BY JOHN RYDELL III

💎 Don't take yourself too seriously.

I wear a terrible wig sometimes. People laugh.

Keep things light. People have enough stress already.

♦ Be useful at work.

If you aren't doing anything useful at work, you will eventually not have a job.

If you go on vacation and nobody cares, start finding something more important to do.

Hanging out and accomplishing nothing makes you miserable, guilty, and eventually you'll have no job.

BY JOHN RYDELL III

💎 Arthur Brooks teaches earned success.

People want to earn their success. It's what makes them happy.

Brooks wrote a whole book on it.

💎 The David Brooks Rule:

Make other people feel seen, heard, respected, and understood.

This is hard. Don't focus on yourself. Focus on the other person.

Being good at this helps you create deep connections that can change the world.

From David Brooks, "How to Know a Person."

BY JOHN RYDELL III

♦ Truly care about others and how they feel.

People will forget what you said but they will never forget how you made them feel.

Here's a great interview trick. Ask, "How did that make you feel?"

◆ Make your personality feel like you are someone's friend.

Good podcasters make you feel like you know them and you are their friend.

The Smartless guys joke around and let you into their lives.

Pat Mayo, Geoff Fienberg, and Tim Anderson talk sports but people care more about them.

Rob Bell makes everyone feel like they know him.

So let your guard down. Be vulnerable. Let people know you and feel like an insider.

BY JOHN RYDELL III

💎 Be the best in your category/niche.

Keep narrowing your focus until you can be the best.

No business ever succeeds by trying to be mediocre and getting 1% of a generic market.

◆ Be a great part of your community...

Whatever virtual or physical community you are part of, be a good member.

Help your industry, or your town, or your association.

In return, your community will be there for you when you need them.

BY JOHN RYDELL III

💎 Patients in hospitals need help.

If you are in a hospital, find an unemotional advocate to help you.

Hospitals can save your life but they can also be very dangerous.

Whenever possible, make sure someone is checking the doctors, medications, and nurses.

Be the nicest and most thankful patient but check everything with your advocate.

◈ Whenever possible, buy large deductible insurance plans.

Take the small risks that you can afford.

Use insurance for the catastrophic losses that you can't afford.

Remember that your insurance broker is a salesperson who gets paid more if you spend more.

BY JOHN RYDELL III

♦ Business travel is expensive.

Make sure you keep an eye on travel and entertainment expenses.

But don't get so cheap that important people are miserable on the road.

Use sites like CostCoTravel.com and AAA for fair values if you aren't big enough to negotiate corporate deals.

◆ Attend conferences only when there is an ROI.

When someone is planning to attend a conference, make sure there is an ROI on the attendance.

And don't just count the hard costs of attending an event. Count the time and opportunity costs as well.

BY JOHN RYDELL III

♦ You don't always need to buy fancy real estate.

I have a friend who once bought a hotel that I thought was a mediocre property.

He usually bought high end properties. So I was confused.

Until he reminded me that he buys hotels based on the spreadsheet numbers and financial returns.

Not based on what they look like.

💎 Maximize your credit card points.

If you are lucky enough to have a small business, then make sure you maximize your points.

But never ever use a credit card for debt. The interest rates are too high!

BY JOHN RYDELL III

💎 The Rick Mercer Rule:

Achieve Economic Freedom.

Figure out how to get to a place where you work because you want to, not because you have to.

It isn't just about how much money you have in the bank.

When work isn't a burden, life gets amazing.

💎 The Don Chambers Rule:

You need to double your income to afford a 10% lifestyle increase.

Most people make a bit more money and then think they can live like the "rich" people.

It seems crazy but you need to double your income if you want to improve your lifestyle by 10%.

BY JOHN RYDELL III

💎 Maximize your retirement plan.

Make sure you are putting as much into your retirement plan as possible.

Usually you get a match, tax savings, and compounded growth.

Very small businesses can also often find some very creative and legal solutions to really boost their tax efficient retirement savings.

💎 Spend less money than you make.

Always. (Or at least until you retire.)

BY JOHN RYDELL III

💎 Go upstream to fix problems.

For more information, read the parable of the river.

If you keep needing to solve the same problem over and over, look upstream.

Fix the problems upstream, and you won't spend so much time fixing problems later.

💎 KYC - Know your customers.

There is almost no industry left where you can get away with not knowing your customers.

Know who they are. Be proud of them. Kick the bad apples out.

That should help you stay away from trouble.

BY JOHN RYDELL III

♦ Hire people better than you.

This can be a hard one for super talented people.

Even if you find someone better than you "at some things" that is great.

They don't have to be better than you at everything.

If you do find someone great, take good care of them and never lose them.

◆ When it comes to diversity, remember MLK, Jr's dream:

"I have a dream that my four little children will one day live in a nation where they will not be judged by the color of their skin but by the content of their character."

BY JOHN RYDELL III

💎 Create equal opportunities.

The goal of equality should be to create equal opportunities.

Equality should not strive for equal outcomes for all.

Give people as much opportunity to thrive as possible, then let them compete for success.

◆ No drama at work.

If you have employees that constantly create drama, then tell them to stop or get rid of them.

Once you have worked in a drama-free environment, you'll never go back.

BY JOHN RYDELL III

💎 Money motivates people.

People run organizations, companies, and the government.

Want to understand why decisions are being made?

Follow the money.

It is often that simple.

💎 Make backups.

When you have backups you don't need them.

When you have good data backups and contingency plans, you never seem to need them.

When you skimp on these things, you always need them.

I don't know why this works.

BY JOHN RYDELL III

◆ **My favorite church.**

Our Lady of the Rocks is an amazing church in Montenegro.

It can teach you:

Adventure

Gratitude for safety.

Building one stone (or hair) at a time.

The massive value of a safe harbor.

◆ Wake up grateful.

People with gratitude are happier.

Be grateful for another day.

Be grateful for what you have.

BY JOHN RYDELL III

◆ Don't talk behind peoples' backs.

If you have feedback for someone, tell them to their face.

Don't build a culture that allows chatter about people behind their backs.

💎 Don't play telephone when giving feedback.

If someone comes to you with feedback about a colleague, do everything possible to convince them to share it directly with the primary person.

Otherwise, you end up sharing feedback in a very awkward way without enough direct information and examples.

And the person receiving the feedback usually knows who is giving the feedback anyway.

BY JOHN RYDELL III

💎 Even Bill Russell likes encouragement.

Everyone wants to hear that they are doing a good job.

Bill once said that he didn't get enough feedback in college while playing basketball.

His coach thought he was so good that he didn't need feedback. Wrong.

Everyone wants to hear they are doing a good job.

◆ Dodger baseball manager Tommy Lasorda used to say,

"There are three kinds of people in the world:

People who make it happen,

People who watch what happens,

And people who wonder what happened."

BY JOHN RYDELL III

💎 Make decisions based on data... not emotions.

If you have great data and great intuition, you can go far.

◆ You better figure out how AI can help you.

Don't get caught up in the hype.

Get focused on what it can actually DO to help you, your team, and your customers be more efficient.

Don't wait.

BY JOHN RYDELL III

💎 $10, $100, $1000 hourly work.

How much time are you spending doing each type of work?

How can you stop doing $10/hr work and start doing $1,000/hr work?

Get the most value out of your day!

Programmers should be programming.

Writers should be writing.

Producers should be producing.

Don't let them spend 50% of their time on meetings and activities that are worthless.

BY JOHN RYDELL III

💎 Remember that everyone has too much to do.

Everyone and every company is resource constrained.

So make sure you know your priorities and say no often.

💎 Don't forget the cost of tending your gardens.

Planting a garden has a cost.

Caring for it has a recurring cost forever.

The same is true when you build software.

Don't forget about the recurring costs of tending your gardens!

BY JOHN RYDELL III

◈ Passive income is magical.

Create investments, businesses, or projects that pay you even when you aren't working.

The truly wealthy people in life don't trade their time for money.

💎 Don't hit "reply all" to an email unless you really need to.

BCC people. Don't cc them all.

People who cc a ton of people or reply to a ton of people waste millions of hours!

BY JOHN RYDELL III

💎 Who else needs to know something?

Every time you send an email try to think who else might need the info.

And cc them on the email. Or send it to them as an FYI.

You can keep someone up to speed with an extra few seconds.

But do NOT overdo it.

♦ Send fewer emails.

Try to send emails that cover everything and don't need a lot of back and forth.

If you can send an email with full instructions it will save everyone a ton of time.

"I'm available at 2pm or 4pm on Monday. If that works for you, please send a calendar hold with a Zoom link and I'll be there."

BY JOHN RYDELL III

◆ Don't send angry emails.

If an email thread is going on and on or people are getting angry, STOP replying.

Jump on a phone call and get things resolved.

Long, angry, emotional emails never help. Ever.

Be quick to apologize and to admit your mistakes.

The buck stops with you. Always.

BY JOHN RYDELL III

💎 Changing people is hard.

People can change habits incrementally.

But is it very, very hard to change who someone is at the fundamental level.

If you need dramatic change from someone in your life, you should be realistic about what is possible and what isn't.

💎 Ray Dalio's culture advice:

"Create a culture in which it is ok to make mistakes and unacceptable not to learn from them."

BY JOHN RYDELL III

◆ Do you need an obsessed person to have massive success?

i.e. Steve Jobs and Elon Musk.

Entrepreneurs are difficult at best and abrasive at worst.

How do you blend these attributes to change the world?

💎 Give your staff opportunities, but be realistic.

Not everyone can be the CEO. Not everyone wants to be.

Some people are likely going to be doing their job at their level forever.

So help people set goals but don't mislead people into thinking they will grow into positions that are unattainable.

BY JOHN RYDELL III

💎 Don't lie.

You will lose people's trust.

And you'll get caught in your own web of lies and won't even remember what is true anymore.

◆ Be flexible to get more.

When you are negotiating for something, don't dig in your heels or get too specific.

If the other party needs your buy-in to proceed, then be flexible about what you want.

They will often find win/win scenarios where you will get a lot more than if you just asked for something specific.

And they will see you as a partner.

BY JOHN RYDELL III

💎 Negotiate on 4 quadrants.

Car salespeople have 4 ways to make money:

Car price, trade-in price, add-ons, and finance/insurance.

They don't care which quadrant makes them money.

If your customer wants a good deal in one aspect of your pricing, make it up elsewhere.

💎 Custom software is too expensive.

I'm a programmer. My team writes custom software.

But building software is hard and expensive.

Don't ever build custom software if you can avoid it.

Buy everything possible off-the-shelf and spend time integrating it.

BY JOHN RYDELL III

💎 Turn every major project into the smallest useful nugget.

Then get those nuggets done.

That way you get value fast even if the overall project gets derailed.

◆ Use sprints to get stuff done.

They don't have to be complicated.

You don't need lots of rules and methods.

Just set a short deadline, hustle, and get stuff done.

Urgency helps achieve great things.

BY JOHN RYDELL III

♦ Cyber attacks are a massive global problem.

The federal government isn't going to do anything to protect you.

Make sure you have insurance and then do everything possible to ensure you never need it.

♦ Projects, time, and money.

Almost everything in life takes more time and costs more money than you expect.

Build contingencies when creating time and financial budgets.

The bigger the project, the worse it gets.

If you can find someone who will do a fixed-price contract, go for it!

BY JOHN RYDELL III

💎 Don't use a semi truck to deliver the groceries.

Don't make things too complicated.

Don't overbuild.

Keep it simple.

◆ Bad processes or bad people?

If something is going wrong, make sure that you don't have a process problem.

Sometimes good people fail due to bad processes.

BY JOHN RYDELL III

💎 Test before you hire.

Give people test projects or short consulting projects before hiring them.

This isn't always possible, but you learn more working with someone than you possibly can from an interview or a recommendation.

◈ Worst omelet chef ever.

This is the story of the amazing omelet chef who was accidentally destroying an entire hotel:

I was visiting a high end hotel in Hawaii that included a breakfast buffet.

There was a super friendly and careful omelet station chef who did a great job and made people smile.

But he was 2-3x slower than his colleagues.

HIs slowness caused the line to stretch so long that people couldn't navigate the buffet.

This caused massive wait times for guests to be seated in the restaurant and everyone started their day upset at the hotel.

All due to one friendly, careful omelet maker.

BY JOHN RYDELL III

♦ Create magical ice cream.

Make ice cream by soaking the milk in breakfast cereal.

This is awesome because the ice cream tastes great and makes you feel like a kid.

It is a sneaky example of caring so much that you take your craft to the next level.

💎 Care deeply about your customers.

Want a great example of a fictional restaurant that really, really cares?

Watch The Bear TV Show; Season 2, Episode 7.

Can you build a business that cares *that* much about your customers?

BY JOHN RYDELL III

◆ Sylvestor Stalone's dog.

Legend has it that Sylvester Stalone sold his dog because he so passionately wanted to create Rocky.

One, think how much he cared?

Two, when you burn all of the ships in the harbor, you have no choice left but to succeed.

Go all in.

💎 Model James Cameron.

James Cameron would create movies and scenes that *he* wanted to watch.

It turns out that what he wanted to watch was true for millions of others.

Create services and art that you love and others will also.

BY JOHN RYDELL III

◆ Emotional emotions.

I heard this during a sporting event the other day:

"Play with emotion but don't become emotional."

Seems like a great way to act at work as well.

Care enough to do your job with passion and emotion.

But don't become emotional and let your emotions get in your way of having fun and success.

♦ The General Patton Rule:

"He who sweats more in training, bleeds less in battle."

Apply this to exercise.

Apply it to preparing for anything you do.

BY JOHN RYDELL III

💎 In a crisis, you don't have to know exactly what to do.

Be calm, over-communicate, and be direct about what you need.

The reason you exercise is so that you can remain calm in an emergency and slow your breathing.

💎 Say thank you to people.

Always.

Genuinely.

Don't forget.

BY JOHN RYDELL III

💎 Always be willing to change your mind.

If you are going down the wrong path, then stop a project as soon as you know it is wrong.

Cut your losses before you make them a lot bigger.

💎 The Rock says:

"True confidence is being able to change your mind."

BY JOHN RYDELL III

💎 Have a fast cadence for your company.

Consistently choose to get more done.

Book meetings for tomorrow — not for two weeks from now.

But never make up false deadlines that just ruin people's lives.

♦ Porn drives technology.

Porn brought us:

Videotapes – movies you can watch at home.

The internet with fast streaming.

Secure online payments.

Digital cameras

Virtual reality

New tech innovations are often initially driven by porn (sex), which drives prices down and leads to mass adoption.

BY JOHN RYDELL III

💎 Never take your eye off the core of your business.

Don't just go through the motions.

Don't forget about the basics.

Measure, monitor, review, and care passionately about the core – not the fluff.

◆ Find people who are great at saying no.

Sometimes saying no is much more important than saying yes.

BY JOHN RYDELL III

💎 Get rid of the bottom 10%.

Every company can cut the bottom 10% of the workforce.

Don't miss out on those opportunities.

And if you work at a company that cuts the bottom 10%, don't be worried.

They won't cut you if you are a top performer.

💎 Mediocre people bring down a whole company.

It isn't just that they are mediocre.

It creates a culture where their peers realize that it is ok to be mediocre.

It isn't.

BY JOHN RYDELL III

◆ Have others own your ideas.

Try to always make someone believe that an idea is theirs and not yours.

Someone once told me I was "tricking" people into thinking my ideas were theirs.

That isn't a trick. That's building consensus and ownership.

💎 The Bus Factor:

Make sure that there is nobody on your team who is the only person who can do something.

The same goes for you.

If there are things that nobody else can do, then train someone else.

At least create narrated screen recordings of complex stuff you do that someone can watch in a pinch.

BY JOHN RYDELL III

⬥ **Nobody is irreplaceable.**

It is always surprising how easy it is for organizations to move on even when someone "really important" is gone.

Don't overvalue yourself or others.

◆ Big government doesn't solve problems.

Big companies don't either:

"... If money could solve problems, the government would be accomplishing wonders."

Elon Musk. June 24, 2023 tweet.

BY JOHN RYDELL III

💎 Long-term deficit spending destroys countries.

If your government leaders are spending money with no plans to pay it back then then they are stealing from future generations.

If you love your children and grandchildren, why are you making them pay off your debt?

Stop being selfish. Do what is right for those who come after you.

💎 Hire people in small towns.

Don't hire people in expensive anti-business cities and states.

It isn't worth the hassle and people who live in expensive places usually have financial stress.

If you have the luxury of hiring remotely, use that to your advantage.

But don't pay people in equivalent jobs less just because they live somewhere cheap.

Celebrate them.

BY JOHN RYDELL III

◆ **Negotiate whenever you can.**

Sometimes people forget to negotiate mortgages, loans, insurance, etc.

There can be massive differences between similar products.

Make sure you always have at least two people bidding for your business.

♦ Use independent advisors.

Find independent financial advisors, mortgage brokers, and insurance agents.

Whenever possible, have someone advising you who is independent and can sell any brand.

And make sure you understand how they are getting paid so you know their biases.

BY JOHN RYDELL III

◆ Cash is King.

People and businesses who have cash have a huge competitive advantage.

You don't waste your time creating reports for bankers and you don't waste money paying interest.

If you have cash, don't forget your competitive advantage and leverage it.

♦ Vin Scully's final words on air:

"May God give you for every storm, a rainbow,

For every tear, a smile,

For every care, a promise,

And a blessing in each trial.

For every problem life sends,

A faithful friend to share.

For every sigh, a sweet song,

And an answer for every prayer."

BY JOHN RYDELL III

💎 Eb Shortle:

My best friend growing up had an amazing father who passed away recently.

They wrote this about him in his obituary.

"Eb was a sweet and gentle soul, thoughtful and kind, intelligent and wise, competent and reliable, humble, supportive and loving."

This isn't exaggerated. What will people say when you are gone?

♦ Be a generational leader.

Author Nelson Henderson writes,

"The true meaning of life is to plant trees, under whose shade you do not expect to sit."

Have a long-term vision for your life.

Make a generational impact.

BY JOHN RYDELL III

💎 A riff on Proverbs 26:7.

"Nothing is more useless than wise sayings said by people who don't ever apply them to their own lives.

Wisdom only becomes wisdom as it is applied, not memorized.

Fools would rather be well read than well lived."

Jason Jaggard's Ancient Riffs.

https://ancientriffs.substack.com/

♦ Finish Strong.

Always sprint across the finish line.

Never cut corners at the very end.

You came this far.

Finish the job.

BY JOHN RYDELL III

💎 Please send me an email.

I finished reading a great book the other day.

When I got to the end, I wished I had a way to thank the author and maybe even provide some feedback.

So here you go. You can find me at jrydell@gmail.com.

I Hope to hear from you.

ACKNOWLEDGEMENTS

I have to thank numerous people who helped to make this book a reality. Without their help, this book would simply not exist. To my Mom and Dad, who not only provided me with much wisdom growing up, but who also helped me edit this book. To my wife, Lisa, who has been my partner for the past 34 years and whose opinions, experiences, and love have helped shape much of this book. To my children, John Otto, and Alexa, who have listened to their dad's crazy ideas for their whole lives, To Rachel Hechter, who continues to provide amazing assistance with my writing and has been a great member of our team for more than 20 years. To Chris Sorensen, my friend and CEO of PhoneBurner, who works tirelessly on our business and constantly inspires me with his wisdom. To my brother, and business partner, Paul Rydell, who has been an amazing partner for many decades. To Johnny Horter, my very young friend, who accidentally read the very first draft of this book in one sitting, and gave me the inspiration to get it finished. To all of my friends, colleagues, and family who have supported me along the way. And to all of the very wise people whose ideas formed many of the "little gems" in this book. Thank you!

Made in the USA
Columbia, SC
16 July 2024

e9209300-5e1c-4efe-9086-1d83c8bdada5R01